Beloved Dog

Beloved Dog

MAIRA KALMAN

PENGUIN PRESS

NEW YORK

2015

For My Beloved Children

LBK and AOK

When I go out for a WALK,
there is So MUch I SEE
that makes me HAPPy to
be ALIVE. BReathing.
Not ThinKing. ObseRving.
I am gRAteFuL beyond measuRe
to bE PARt of it ALL.
There aRe PEOPLe, of COURSE,
heRoic and hEARTBReaKing,
going about their business
in splendid fAShion.

There Are the
Discarded items—
Chairs, Sofas,
Tables, Umbrellas,
Shoes—
Also heroic for
having lived life
in happy (or unhappy)
homes.

There are TREES.
GLORIOUS and CONSOLING.
Changing with the Seasons.
Reminders that ALL things
Change. And change Again.
There are FLOWERS, Birds,
BABIES, Buildings.
I LOVE ALL of these.
BUT ABOVE ALL, I AM BESOTTED
by DOGS.

You, READING this book,
Most likely hAVE,
oR had, A dog.
You ceRtainly Know that
youR doG is, oR WAS, the
DEAREST, FUNNiEST,
LoVingest, LoYALEST
FRiend you EVER had.

YOUR eager playmate.

YOUR FRESH-AIR companion.

YOUR ANCHOR.

YOUR
PRIDE.

YOUR MUSE.

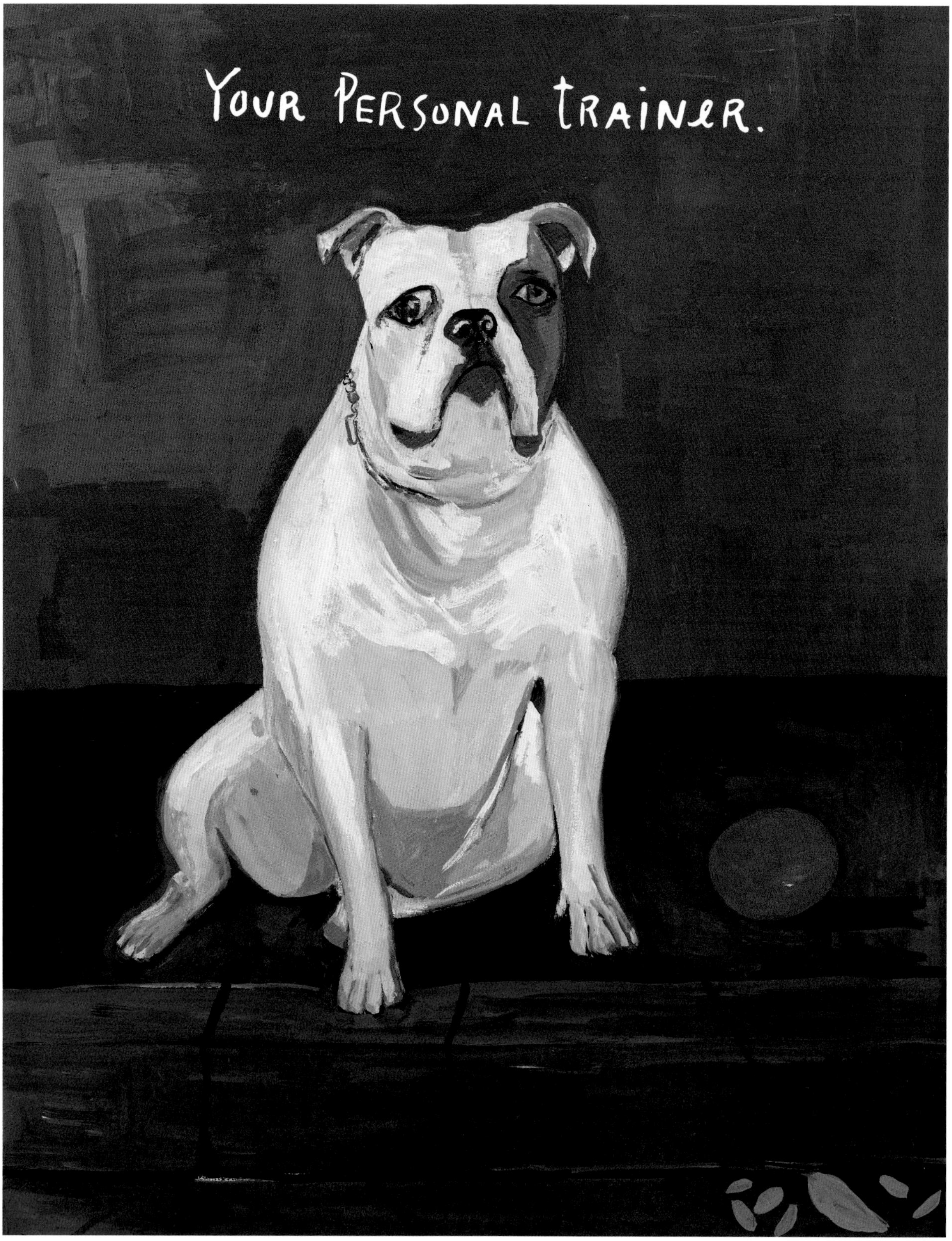
YOUR PERSONAL TRAINER.

YOUR BABY.

Your antidepressant.
Your ZOLOFT.
Literally,
this Dog's name
is
ZOLOFT.

Your family.

Your solace.

Your savior.

Your pal.

When I look through decades of my work, I am amazed and amused to realize the extent of my fixation. Dogs appear everywhere, whether they belong to the story or not. They always make me laugh and warm my heart.

But it was not always like that.

BEFORE I had a dog, I was terrified of all DOGS, BiG and SMALL. EVERYONE KNEW they were NOT To BE TRUSTED, and that if you TURNed youR HEAd AWAY foR ONE iNSTANT, A DOG WOULD LUNGE at YOUR THROAT and RIP youR HEAd OFF.

At LEAST, thAT WAS what my MOTHER TAught me.

SAME DOG

My Mother's family came from BelaRus. A bunch of shacks on the River Sluch. My grandmother was terrified of dogs and was obsessed with cleanLiness. Everything had to sparkle and shine. No Room for dogs in the SHACK.

It was the same for my mother when we moved to the BRONX. OuR apartment was as spARKLing and shiny as the SHACK. But here we Read VOGUE, and LIFE magazine. There were pages with BEAUTIFUL people in BeAutiFuL Homes with MULTipLE Dogs.

WHO WERE THESE PEOPLE? DID THEIR dogs NOT smell

OR SHED? OR LUNGE at THEIR NECKS?

YEARS passed.

At college I fell in love with a Hungarian man named Tibor.

He was curious about my purple polka-dot miniskirt. I was curious about his leather jacket and pack of cigarettes. He wanted to shut down the university and overthrow the government. Which He did not.

I wanted to write tortured poetry in Bohemian cafés and knit him a RED sweater. Which I did.

One day he took me to meet his parents. His parents had a dog.

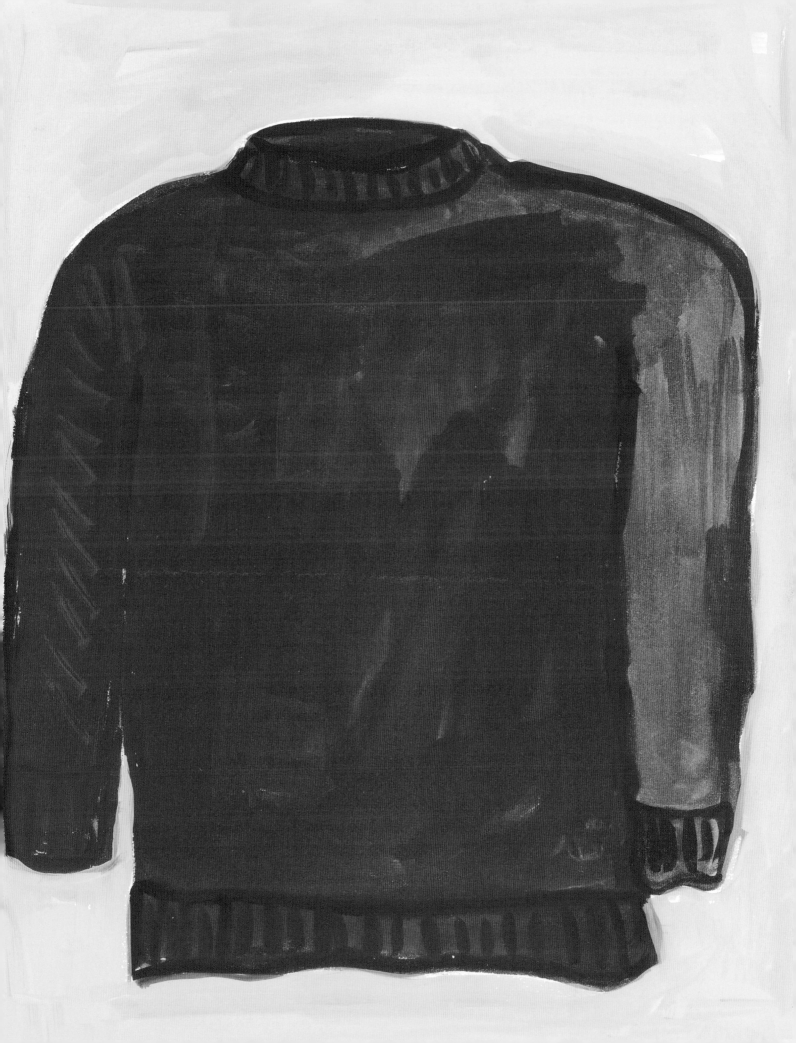

A BIG BLACK SLOBBERING HAIRY HUNGARIAN BEAST NAMED BOGANCH. I KEPT A polite distANCE (fRom the DOG and the PARENTS). A tENSE PAT on the HEAd (of the DOG) WAS ALL I COULd MUSTER.

It took A LOT of ALERTNESS Not to tURN My BACK on that DOG. He WAS hungRy looKing and CERTAINLY ReSented the FACT That I spoKE no HungaRiaN. IN my deFENSE, HungaRiaN is a VERY diFFiCULt LANguAge to LEARn.

The years passed. I married Tibor.
We had two children. We had fun
and LOVE and disagreements (fights)
and travel. We worked together and
created things. The children were
splendid children and though
sometimes (or often) someone
was mad at someone, we ALL
loved each other madly.
And then one disastrous DAY,
my husband fell ill.
My beloved, LARGER-than-life,
indomitable husband was
going to die.

Someone had an idea.
Get a dog.

And I thought,
"Well, that's NOT going to happen.
In the struggle of life and
Death, in the world of shattered
hopes, some things could
not change. NO DOG."
But then, with an INEXPLICABLE
About-FACE, some remote part
of my brain acknowledged that
this might be a good thing for
the children. And I said YES.

He WAS an IRish Wheaten, the coloR
of piNK champagne. We named him
PETE.
I WAS AFRAid to touch him.
And tHeN, Little by LittLE - oR
perhaps with blinding speed - I
fell madly in LOVE.
WE took WALKS togetheR and
stopped ofTen to tALK to pEOplE,
oR juST Look ARound.
He stayed next to me the ENTiRE
DAy and SLEPT on the FLooR
NExt to My BEd.

He modeled for me in outfits that tested his patience.

He became the subject of my work. He did what everyone said he would do. Help to keep us as sane and as happy as we could be. Quite an extraordinary achievement.

But nothing special for a dog.

When TiBoR died,
the WORLd
came to An End.
And the WORLd
Did Not
come to An END.
That
is something
You LEARN.

Eight years later, when Pete got sick, we kept him going and going, unable to say good-bye. He died on New Year's Day. The city was QUIET, muffled under a blanket of fluffy white snow. It seems fitting to end with this passage from James Joyce's "The Dead."

"...the snow falling faintly through the UNIVERSE and faintly falling, like the descent of their last end, upon all the living and the dead."

This book is a compendium of, and tribute to, the Many DOGS I have encountered over the years, in Life and in Books.

They are Constant Reminders that Life Reveals the Best of itself when we Live fully in the moment and Extend our unconditional Love. And it is Very true, that the most Tender, uncomplicated, most generous part of our Being blossoms, without any effort, when it comes to the Love of a DOG.

A
SELECTION
of
PAGES
From
BOOKS
and
MAGAZINES
1986 to the PRESENT

**Mommy had
a little baby.**

There he is
fast asleep.

See him drink
from a bottle.

See him eat
from a plate.

big story

A very big woman
in a red dress
walked down the street
with three cross-eyed dogs.

When the dogs saw a yellow car
they started to bark.
The barking woke Aunt Ida,
who immediately started to sing.
The singing woke Uncle Morris,
who immediately started
to dance.

green hat

The three cross-eyed dogs
felt hungry.
They went to a fancy restaurant
and got a good table.

At the restaurant
a woman in a green hat
took a picture of a man
in a blue suit
while flowers sat
on the table
and smelled so sweet.

tiptoe story

Aunt Ida and Uncle Morris had a dog
named Max.
Max wanted to live in Paris
and be a poet.
In the evening,
Max would tiptoe
down the hall, with a suitcase,
trying to sneak out of the house.
Ida would say to Morris,
"Quick, Morris,
catch the dog."

the poem of max

Max felt blue,
He went to the café
and ordered black coffee and biscuits.
He wrote down a poem
that went like this.

"Dig that boy
with the box
on his head.
Is he buying bread?
Is his name Fred?
And that tall noodle woman
with the polka-dot shoes—
have you ever seen
a nose so red?"

Call me Max.

Max the dreamer.

Max the poet.

Max the dog.

My dream is to live in Paris.

To live in Paris and be a p o e t.

Paris.
The city of dreams.
The city of lights.
The city of love.

But
d o
y o u
think it
is easy
for a dog
to pack a
small brown
suitcase, put
on a beret,
and hop on a
plane? Ha! Plane
tickets cost
money. Mazuma, shekels,
semolians. I have none.
Because no one
wants to buy my
book. I'm flat broke.

Bone dry.

But someday,
fat families and
skinny families
around the world
will be reading my poems.
And laughing, and crying.
I feel it in my bones.

I want to say, before anything,
that dreams
are very important.

I live with Ida and Morris Stravinsky in the spacious Stravinsky apartment. Morris has a ladies' shoe store. Stravinsky Shoes. Every day he goes down to his store and shows women different shoes. Pumps. Sandals. Slippers. Mules. Morris and his assistant Laura are designing shoes for the Queen of Sheba, who must be a very fussy woman, because every time a customer makes Morris crazy he says, "Who do you think you are, the Queen of Sheba?"

mpadour

nuthin

schnozolla

luna

lucky
lemon

Meanwhile, across town,
Ida is taking tango lessons
with Maurice Chagall.

He has a big black shiny
pompadour on his head
and tiny
shiny
pointy shoes
on his feet.

Dearest people,
How can I thank you.

This is the day
I have been waiting for
all my life. I am off.

Off to Paris to follow my dreams.
Be brave, Ida and Morris.
We will meet again
in that starry-eyed city.
You know I have always
lived by my dreams.
And now they have come true.
Roots and wings.
Roots and wings.
I've got to go,
Daddy-o.

So long.
Farewell.
Good-bye.

Ha!

OOH LA LA! (MAX IN LOVE)

Allo? Allo Jacques?
Jacques, it is me, Mimi.
Oui. Oui. Mimi. I just got off
the phone with Kiki.
Oh Jacques, not Fifi, Kiki.
Listen. Zouzou called Loulou,
Loulou called Coco,
Coco called Kiki,
and Kiki called me me.
Have you heard the latest?
Tout Paris is abuzz. Max is here!
Who is Max??? Mon dieu!
Sacre bleu! He is the coolest cat,
I mean the hottest dog.
He is Max Stravinsky.
The dog poet from New York.
That bohemian beagle. He's
staying at Madame Camembert's.
I don't know what he's going
to do, but I will call Tarte.
Tarte Tatin. She finds out
everything from that bogus
Barcelonian baron,
Federico de Potatoes,
who is a fortune hunter or
a fortune teller or something,
but he is très intelligent and
he always gives her the scoop.
Alors, I must run.
My soufflé is sinking.
Jacques, there is something
in the air. Don't you think?

To inhale leafy lilacy Paris.

It was April after all.

A baguette here,
a Napoleon there,

and I continued my ambling

around my

dove gray

debonnaire

town.

As I left the museum,
I saw a scene that made my heart stand still.
A man had written poems all over
the sidewalk and the buildings and the cars
and the trees. As the cars left, parts of
his poems went whizzing around Paris,

and as the leaves fell from the trees,
words fluttered down to the ground.

I kept walking.
I was in a funny mood.
Expecting something I couldn't name.

"Allo Jacques. It's moi, Mimi.
What a horrible day.
The butcher delivered
the wrong order.
Instead of sixty spicy saucisson
and a small steak
for my dog Sutzi
they delivered sixty steaks
and one sweet saucisson.
Then Louis L'Amour came over
and cried for three hours
about his beloved Lula Fabula
who ran away with the circus
to become a snake charmer.
Quelle kook.
But the latest on Max. He has
been seen everywhere with a
hangdog expression on his face
and if I know anything,
which I do,
this moody meandering means
one thing.
Love, Jacques. L'amour.
He is looking for,
needy of, and pining for love.
Lovelovelovelove is in the air.
Isn't it glorious, Jacques?
But I must dash.
My mousse is melting.
Byebye."

The rest, as they say,
is history. Crêpes is
coming with me to Hollywood.
She will compose
the music for my movie.
Our last day in Paris
we led the Dog Day Parade.
I read the poem I had
written for this occasion:
In chic Paree
the chicest day
is when the dogs stroll down
the Champs Elysées.
Great danes romancing,
pink poodles prancing.
It's swank
it's grand
it's pooch couture.
They saunter with style
about half a mile
and end up at Maxims,
that most marvelous spot
for champagne and caviar
and a little whatnot.
A toast to life
A toast to love
Salut! Olé!
We're off to L.A.!

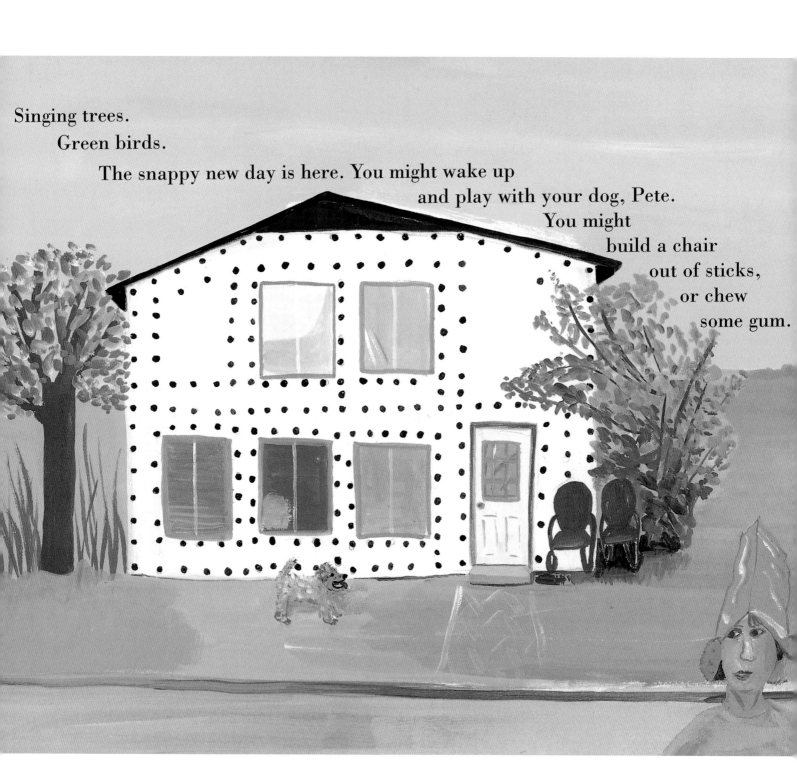

Singing trees.
  Green birds.
    The snappy new day is here. You might wake up
        and play with your dog, Pete.
          You might
              build a chair
                out of sticks,
                  or chew
                    some gum.

You might do
nothing
at
all.

But

while
you
are
sitting
there,
there is a place
in New York City that
is the busiest, fastest, biggest
place there is.
It is a train station.
This place is called
Grand Central.

One day you might (you must) go there.

It's not called grand for nothing!
Everything about it is grand! huge! **monumental!**
Grand staircases.
Polished marble floors.
Stupendous star-filled
ceilings.

Don't take
my picture

Every
day 500,000
people walk, run,
dash, rush — criss-crossing
on and off trains.
It is such a madhouse, people say
IT'S LIKE GRAND CENTRAL IN HERE!
How does it work?
Who does what?
What does
who?

Woof

This is
the room
of all
importance.

Mr. Frank
Chidester
runs the
Lost and Found.
If you lose a red button,
or a suitcase full of diamonds,
or your false teeth,
chances are Mr. Chidester
will have them.
Most lost things
don't bark, but

once…

...once
the absent
minded
Mrs. Clarence
Pffafenburger was
bringing her show dog
Mitzi from Darien
to Greenwich for a
tea party. When
Mrs. Pffafenburger
got off at Greenwich,
she realized
to her horror
that she
had left
Mitzi on
the train.

Good bye Mitzi

But not for long.
Mr. Chidester found Mitzi
and sent her home.
On her own private train.

It's 6:00 p.m. In Vanderbilt Hall…
(It was Mr. Vanderbilt who had the place
built in 1903 after all)… there is a lively celebration going on.
The singer Olga Shmedvig is
singing. When she hits her
high notes people think
it is the train whistle
and start running
for the train.

"my kneeeee

this is
fascinating

Herbert Moosehump is having
fun and so is little Ervin Pil who
will grow up to
be a famous
scientist
because
he eats
beets
every
day!

My name is Poppy Wise.

This is my little brother MOOKIE

and this is my dog PETE.

A good dog.
A VERY GOOD DOG.
But sometimes he is not
so good. He eats what he
should NOT. WHAT?
I will start with A.

a   A   a

apple

He ate
cousin Rocky
accordion.

All of it.

b   B   b

He ate a bouncing
ball that belonged
to uncle Bennie's
dog Buster.

(Buster is no bargain. He barks
            all the time,
            but still...)

Bennie lived in a beautiful room that had a Bed, a Book, a Box, and a Bottle of water.

(And some other things that don't begin with B.)

At the Lucky Dog Show, he ate all the leashes which let loose all

the dogs who ate all the lemon tarts and drank all the lemonade, and Mrs. Parsley was LIVID.

Buster says, "Nuts to Pete."

Now Bennie has no money (NONE) to buy Buster a new ball which, you will remember, Pete ate many letters ago.

n N n

The Twinkle Twins have a dog named Twinky. Twinky may look insane, but she does not eat their things.

LOOKING AT LINCOLN

ONE DAY,
WHILE WALKING THROUGH THE PARK
ON MY WAY TO BREAKFAST
I SAW A VERY TALL MAN.
HE REMINDED ME OF SOMEONE,
BUT I COULD NOT THINK WHO.

He had a family that he loved very much.
His wife, Mary (who was very short), and four sons.
They laughed and had lots of friends and
even ran around a little wild.

I WONDER IF MARY AND ABRAHAM
hAd NICKNAMES FOR EACH OTHER.
DID SHE CALL HIM LINKY?
DID HE CALL HER LITTLE PLUMPY?
MAYBE.

Abe worked hard and
became interested in the government.
He decided he would run for president.
And on March 4, 1861,
he was inaugurated
president of the United States.

ABRAHAM LINCOLN
WILL LIVE FOREVER.
AND IF YOU GO TO
WASHINGTON, D.C.
in the SPRING
YOU CAN WALK

Through the CHERRY BLOSSOMS AND VISIT him.

AT his MEMORIAL YOU CAN READ The WORDS HE WROTE NEAR THE End of The WAR.

"... With malice toward none, with charity for all."

And YOU CAN LOOK into his BEAUTIFUL EYES. JUST LOOK.

WORD NUMBER 4:
Dog

The cake in the box is
strawberry shortcake.

13 WORDS

ideas

"Hey, that'll cheer you up,"
says the dog.
"How about we eat it together?"
They sit at the table and
share the cake.

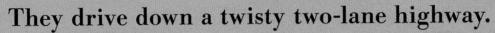

They drive down a twisty two-lane highway.

"So where are we going?" asks the goat.

"Well, the bird is busy painting ladders," says the dog, "but she seems a little sad, even after she ate some cake. I'd like to go find something that might cheer her up."

WORD NUMBER 12: **PANACHE**

The dog has finally chosen one hat for himself and one for the bird. "Both those hats have tons of panache," says the baby, putting them in boxes.

"What does that mean, 'feathers'?" asks the dog.

"Not just feathers," the baby says. "A sense of style and excitement, a kind of verve or swagger. You know what I mean?"

"Yes," says the dog. The goat honks the horn of the convertible.

The dog and the goat drive back home
in the convertible in a state of great excitement.

WELL, SUSAN, THIS IS A FINE MESS YOU ARE IN.

BREAD AND BUTTER WAS ALL SHE SERVED.

NONE OF US IS PERFECT.

E.B. WHITE

WILLIAM STRUNK, JR.

The Dessert

The Lipstick

Sunday afternoon

MEET ME ON THE LAWN

I WANT TO TAKE A PICTURE OF YOU.

VALENTINO'S PUGS, MOLLY AND MAGGIE

A WORD ABOUT
KRUPNIK.
KRUPNIK is A TYPE
oF PoLish SouP.
And the NAME
of this DOG who
I admire very Much.
She LiVES in a Bookstore
in TeL Aviv but Reads Next
to Nothing. She (like Montaigne)
likes herself, and that
is quite enough.

"I AM I BECAUSE my little dog
Knows me." – GeRTRude Stein

"ALL Knowledge,
the totality of all questions
and ALL answers
is contained
in the DOG."

-FRANZ KAFKA

During our years together,
I often asked Pete to say ONE WORD
to me. JUST ONE WORD.
It is like asking to hear one word
from a loved one who has died.
Give me a sign you have not
really left me. It is Not
going to happen. But it does not
stop you from wishing and hoping
for a miracle.
So I would BEG PETE TO SAY
ONE WORD. HE NEVER did.
BUT of COURSE, HE SPOKE VOLUMES.

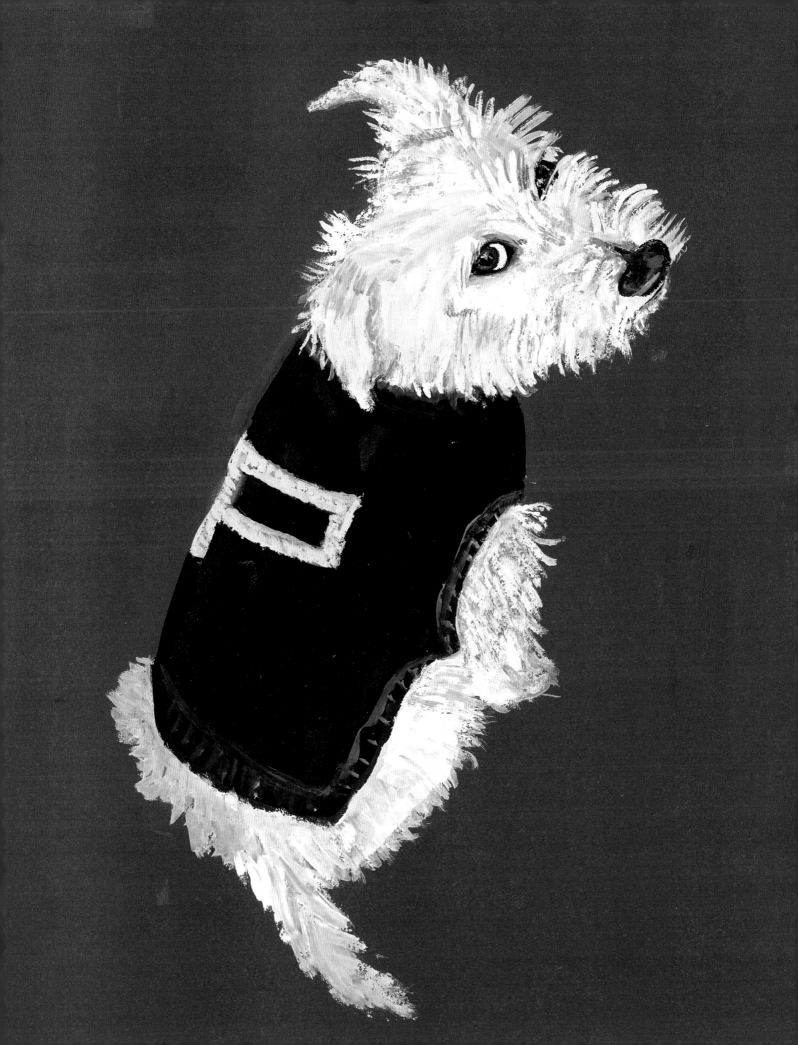

Thank you SPOONER

Thank you BUCKY

(HarperCollins, 2014), *Next Stop, Grand Central* (G. P. Putnam's Sons, 1999), *Ooh-la-la! (Max in Love)* (Viking, 1991), *The Principles of*

for every reader. Some of the artwork first appeared in Maira Kalman's *13 Words*, text by Lemony Snicket (HarperCollins, 2010),

• PENGUIN PRESS · An imprint of Penguin Random House LLC · 375 Hudson Street · New York, New York 10014 · penguin.com

Uncertainty (Penguin Press, 2007), *Stay Up Late*, from a song by David Byrne (Viking, 1987), *What Pete Ate (From A to Z)* (G. P. Putnam's Sons, 2001) and in

The Elements of Style Illustrated, text by William Strunk, Jr. and E. B. White (Penguin Press, 2005), *Food Rules: An Eater's Manual*, text by Michael Pollan

Copyright © 2015 by Maira Kalman · Penguin supports copyright. Copyright fuels creativity, encourages diverse voices, promotes free speech, and creates

woof woof woof   woof woof woof   *My Favorite Things*   BOOK DESIGN BY CLAIRE NAYLON VACCARO.   *Max Makes a Million* (Viking, 1990),   (Nancy Paulsen Books, 2012),   *Looking at Lincoln*   1 3 5 7 9 10 8 6 4 2   (Viking, 1988),   *Pyramids*   Printed in the United States of America ·

scanning, or distributing any part of it in any form without permission. You are supporting writers and allowing Penguin to continue to publish books

(Penguin Press, 2011), *Girls Standing on Lawns*, text by Daniel Handler (Museum of Modern Art, 2014), *Hey Willy, See the*

issues of *Interview*, *The New Yorker*, and *Travel + Leisure*.   LIBRARY OF CONGRESS CATALOGING-IN-PUBLICATION DATA IS AVAILABLE   ISBN: 0-978-1-59420-594-1

Thank you
Vicki